MW01205559

On Eagle's Wings

A Collection of Poems

Lee Underwood

On Eagle's Wings

Scripture quotations used in this book are from the following sources:

The King James Version of the Bible (KJV)

Scripture taken from The Holy Bible,New International Version ® NIV ® Copyright © 1973, 1978, 1984 by International Bible Society. Used by permission of Zondervan Publishing House. All rights reserved.

Scripture taken from The New King James Version. Copyright © 1982 by Thomas Nelson, Inc. Used by permission. All rights reserved.

The Contemporary English Version. (CEV)

PUBLISHED BY:
BRENTWOOD CHRISTIAN PRESS
4000 BEALLWOOD AVENUE
COLUMBUS, GA 31904

Dedicated to: The one who died for me.

But they that wait upon the Lord shall renew their strength; they shall mount up with wings as eagles; they shall run, and not be weary; and they shall walk, and not faint.

Isaiah 40:31

Do not judge, or you too will be judged.

Matthew 7:1

Judge Not

Thank The Lord, it's not my place to Judge,

But that of the most high God above,

A God of tender mercy--love,

Who looks not upon our faces,

But upon our hearts, the secret places,

The dark recesses of our minds,

the bad He knows, the good He finds.

Lord, keep me from Judgments free,

So you'll not mete out the same to me.

When I consider your heavens, the work of your fingers, the moon and the stars, which you have set in place, what is man that you are mindful of him, the son of man that you care for him?

Psalm 8:3-4

Wonders

The sun is rising o'er the hill

According to the Father's will.

The Lord has made this glorious day,

Rejoice, rejoice the psalmists say.

The moon created by God's hand,

Makes of this world a wonder land.

The stars come out, God's candle light,

Oh, what an awesome, wondrous sight.

For this reason a man will leave his father and mother and be united to his wife, and the two will become one flesh. So they are no longer two, but one.

Mark 10:7-8

Not Whole

You went away and part of me went with you,

God's word says man and wife shall be as one.

The parting will always be remembered,

Until God says, "My child, your race is run."

I have my body; my emotions, mind

and spirit make my soul,

But I don't know which part of me is missing,

I do know this, I am no longer whole.

Do not be anxious about anything, but in everything, by prayer and petition, with thanksgiving, present your requests to God.

Philippians 4:6

Away

I thought I couldn't bear to see you go;

It was because I loved you so.

But I put you in my Father's hands;

As you went off to distant lands.

And now I pray while you're away,

When I wake at night, and through the day;

That my Father will keep you in his care,

And I'll have no fear while you are there.

"Whoever does God's will is my brother and sister and mother."

Mark 3:35

Christian Family

I fail in many different ways,

I falter and stumble every day.

Sometimes I wonder, Lord who cares,

Then I hear my Christian brother's prayers.

They ask that you will love and bless

Me, in my sickness, my distress.

Their prayers abound like gentle rain,

They bless, they comfort, they sustain.

I feel your love in their sweet deeds,

In them are met my deepest needs.

Lord, bless my Christian family,

They are so kind, so dear to me.

Keep them in your watch and care,

Always here, forever there.

After Jesus was born in Bethlehem in Judea, during the time of King Herod, Magi from the east came to Jerusalem and asked, "Where is the one who has been born King of the Jews? We saw his star in the east and have come to worship him."

Matthew 2:1

The Star

The star at the top of the Christmas tree

Reminds me of the Wise Men Three,

Who followed a star in search of a child,

And found a savior undefiled.

The one who came to save from sin,

The souls of men to Him to win.

The star at the top of the Christmas tree

Reminds me of the Wise Men Three.

Love is patient, love is kind. It does not envy, it does not boast, it is not proud. It is not rude, it is not self-seeking, it is not easily angered, it keeps no record of wrongs. Love does not delight in evil but rejoices with the truth. It always protects, always trusts, always hopes, always perseveres.

I Corinthians 13:4-7

Love is Kind

Wear my shoes, then tell me how to walk.

Tread my path, then perhaps you will not mock.

Bear my burdens, wear my cross,

Feel my sorrows, share my loss.

Look through my eyes and you will see,

The hand that life has dealt to me.

Then tell me true and do not lie,

How would you walk, if you were I?

For I am convinced that neither death nor life, neither angles nor demons, neither the present nor the future, nor any powers, neither height nor depth, nor anything else in all creation, will be able to separate us from the love of God that is in Christ Jesus our Lord.

Romans 8:38-39

Security

Down in The Valley of Shadow,

Shadow of death for me,

I think I'll go without fearing

For Jesus will be going with me.

This frightening world of turmoil,

Loved ones who have gone on before;

Make me homesick for Heaven,

to dwell on eternity's shore.

To Him who holds my future,

Who will bid me to go or to stay;

His will be done in all things,

This will I earnestly pray.

Psalm 23

The Lord is my shepherd, I shall lack nothing. He
makes me lie down in green pastures, he leads me
beside quiet waters, he restores my soul. He guides
me in paths of righteousness for his name's sake.
Even though I walk through the valley of the
shadow of death, I will fear no evil, for you are with
me; your rod and your staff, they comfort me.

You prepare a table before me in the presence of my
enemies. You annoint my head with oil; my cup
overflows.

Surely goodness and love will follow me all the days
of my life, and I will dwell in the house of the Lord
forever.

The Good Shepherd

The Lord to me a shepherd is.
He is mine and I am His.
Through pastures green, my shepherd leads,
And daily His own flock He feeds.
He leads me by the waters still.
And all my needs He does fulfill.
He restores my soul day by day,
or I would faint along life's way.
He leads me in the paths of right
And stays with me to face the fight.
He leads me through the shadows dim,
I have no fear, I trust in Him.
The table He prepares for me,
Suffices on life's storm-tossed sea.
To overflowing, He fills my cup.
When I stumble, He lifts me up.
His goodness and mercy shall never cease,
He fills my soul with perfect peace.
In the Lord's house, I'll some day dwell,
And hear my shepherd say, "All's well."

Dear friends, let us love one another, for love comes from God. Everyone who loves has been born of God and knows God.

I John 4:7

Love Others

Love self and then you'll see

How wonderful love can be,

For it spreads like ripples in the water

And we can be shaped by the Master Potter.

Love others as we love self,

a commandment we'll surely do,

Knowing that love must begin in me

And love must begin in you.

How great is the love the Father has lavished on us,
that we should be called children of God!

I John 3:1a

Show God's Love

When one loves self, then one can see his many faults,

The empty chambers, the cavernous vaults;

To be filled with radiant and shining love,

So others can see the Father above.

Consider it pure joy, my brothers, whenever you face trials of many kinds, because you know that the testing of your faith develops perseverance. Perseverance must finish its work so that you may be mature and complete, not lacking anything.

James 1:2-4

Sunshine and Shadow

Down in the valley, a sorrow, a tear.

Up on the mountain, laughter so dear;

Through all the raindrops, I see a ray,

That will bring sunshine for me today.

Thank you, dear Father, for the bitter, the sweet,

That we might trust you when darkness we meet,

Through all life's sorrow, and all its pain,

You will send joy to us again.

Thank you for all the things you have given,

For the mansions you've prepared for us in heaven.

Thank you for all the things you've denied,

Knowing it's for good what ere you decide.

In the beginning God created the heavens and the earth.

Genesis 1:1

The God of Creation

The mouth of the river when it reaches the sea,

Is mighty and awesome, a wonder to me.

The towering mountains with snow on their peaks,

The God of creation, His majesty speaks.

The bright colored flowers, exquisitely made,

Their part in creation so proudly displayed.

The raindrops which fall from the heavens above,

Speak of His great and His wonderful love.

The little birds with their sweet singing calls,

The Father takes note of each one that falls.

The stars in the heavens like grains of the sand,

Cannot be counted, except by His Hand.

The sun in its course brings winter to earth,

But then it brings spring and with it rebirth.

The seasons bespeak of the Son from above,

The summer the birth of the one that we love,

The winter, His death nailed to the tree,

And spring, His rising that man might be free.

Oh man His creation, we cannot conceive

The wonders in store for those that believe.

Mary's Song

My soul praises the Lord and my spriit rejoices in God my Savior.

Luke 1:46b-47

My Daughter

Oh God your mercies fill my cup

Full and overflowing.

I'll thank you each day I live

With praises warm and glowing,

For the little girl you sent

That I might be a mother.

It's such a joy, a privilege,

A gift I can't repay,

A sacred trust, oh Lord my God

That I'll remember day by day.

Oh thank you for your blessing sweet,

I bow my Lord at your dear feet.

The King was shaken. He went up to the room over the gateway and wept. As he went, he said: "O my son Absalom! My son, my son Absalom! If only I had died instead of you--O Absalom, my son, my son!"

II Samuel 18:33

My Son

Down in the valley of despair I fell,
Darkness engulfed my soul.
I was as the little lost lamb
That wandered away from the fold.
The burden was more than I could bear,
I thought this must be hell.
But the shepherd came and led me back,
And said in words so true,
You know an all-wise God knows best,
He gave His only son too.
A mother is what I wanted to be,
But someday in eternity
I'll have a little one waiting for me.
A treasure more precious than silver and gold,
A little lamb God took to his fold.
Lord, help me my grief and sorrow hide,
Help me to know he has not died.

He replied, "Because you have so little faith. I tell you the truth, if you have faith as small as a mustard seed, you can say to this mountain, 'Move from here to there' and it will move. Nothing will be impossible for you."

Matthew 17:20-21

So Little Faith

I toss and turn upon my bed,

Because I can't get it in my head,

That God will keep me through the night,

Until He sends the morning light.

Forgive my lack of faith dear God,

My body stays close to the sod,

But my mind rejoices, my heart sings,

And my spirit soars on eagle's wings.

Behold, children are a heritage from the Lord, the fruit of the womb is His reward.

Psalm 127:3

The Special Child

God said,

I looked the world over trying to find,

The very best home for this child of mine.

I saw that she needed the love you would give,

So I sent her to you to love as long as you live.

The blessings you'll receive will be from my hand,

And sometime in glory you'll understand.

"But what about you?" he asked. "Who do you say I am?"
Simon Peter answered, "You are the Christ, the Son of the living God."

Matthew 16:15-16

Our Church

This church was built upon this rock:

"Thou art the Christ , The Son of the Living God."

And my love thanked God that he was a part

Of this church that God built upon this rock.

He is away, he is not here,

To celebrate this church's 50th year.

I asked God to let him stay

So he might celebrate this day.

But he had to go, but in God's plan,

He used my love -- this mortal man.

Her children rise up and call her blessed;

Proverbs 31:28a

Mother

She loved me like no other,

My dear, precious Mother.

She loved me through time past,

Now God has called her home at last,

She'll love me through eternity,

For God has promised her I'll see.

Now faith is being sure of what we hope for and certain of what we do not see.

Hebrews 11:1

Faith

We won't doubt it for a minute,

God's wondrous love and care;

And when we call upon Him,

He's always waiting there.

We won't be anxious about tomorrow,

We won't be filled with doubt and fear,

For He's promised He won't leave us,

He's promised He'll be near.

So we'll go forth amid the conflict,

clothed in the armour He'll provide;

Knowing that He is always with us,

Walking closely by our side.

When did we see you sick or in prison and go to visit you?'
"The King will reply, 'I tell you the truth, whatever you did for one of the least of these brothers of mine, you did for me.'

Matthew 25:39-40

Hospice

May the Lord bless Hospice,
St. Francis is it's name;
If I had a magic wand,
I would cover it with fame.
But God knows of their loving care,
Their many kind, sweet deeds,
that saw us through our darkest hour,
And met our deepest needs.
I am sure they do not seek world fame,
Or temporal things of earth,
But to bring relief in times of grief,
Because of Jesus' birth.
So as you go about your task,
God bless you is my prayer,
that wherever there is a need,
You will be waiting there.

Are not two sparrows sold for one penny? Yet not one of them will fall to the ground apart from the will of your Father. And even the very hairs of your head are all numbered. So don't be afraid; you are worth more than many sparrows.

Matthew 10:29-31

Helping Hands

The cries come from across the land,

Cries of sorrow and despair;

And along you come with helping hands

to let them know somebody cares.

God hears their cries from up above--

The need for someone to show them love.

The one who gives the sparrow feed

Will take note of your sweet deed,

And bless you in unnumbered ways

Until the ending of your days.

For God so loved the world that he gave his one and only Son, that whoever believes in him shall not perish but have eternal life.

John 3:16

Show God's Love

There is a God above,

And His word says He is love;

And He wants us to show this love

to the dying and those in grief,

So they will know how much He cares,

as He works through you to bring relief.

So we thank God for your helping hands,

And God rejoices too,

As you go forth to do a job,

That only you can do.

"Eye has not seen, nor ear heard, nor have entered into the heart of man the things which God has prepared for those who love Him."

I Corinthians 2:9

Rejoice

Rejoice, rejoice a child has gone home,

No more a pilgrim in this world to roam.

But shed tears for your own sorrow and grief;

Because God gave us tears to bring us relief.

"Count it pure joy when you suffer trials."

For God knows and goes with us each weary mile.

In everything, do to others what you would have them do to you, for this sums up the Law and the Prophets.

Matthew 7:12

Do Unto Others

"What you have done unto the least of these my

brethren,

You have done it unto me."

These are the Lord's words, and what we do for

others,

The Lord will surely see.

So we thank God for your helping hands,

And God rejoices too,

As you go forth to do a job,

That only you can do.

The Lord God said, "It is not good for the man to be alone. I will make a helper suitable for him."

Genesis 2:18

Loneliness

As I journey through this land,

I need someone to hold my hand.

My Savior, Jesus, meek and mild,

Seems to ask, "Am I not enough my child?"

And I weep.

Religion that God our Father accepts as pure and faultless is this: to look after orphans and widows in their distress and to keep oneself from being polluted by the world.

James 1:27

The Nursing Home

She needed love, and we had none to give her,

A touch could have dispelled a shadow,

And brought with it a ray of light,

But we went forth blindly and unheeding,

And left her in the shadow without light.

Go forth today into the darkness,

Go with God's radiance in your smile,

And lift some life out of the shadow,

If only for just a little while.

Therefore whoever humbles himself as this little child is the greatest in the kingdom of heaven.

Matthew 18:4

Always Young

There is a little girl inside of me,

That will not go away;

Although my bones creak when I walk,

And my hair is silvery gray.

I hope she always stays with me,

to cheer, to laugh, to play,

to fill my life with sunshine

As I go along life's way.

Set your mind on things above, not on earthly things.

Colossians 3:2

Thanksgiving

God, I thank you for all the things I hold dear;

Your peace, love and comfort,

and your voice of cheer.

Let me hold fast the things upon high,

Things of the earth will soon fade and die.

But store up for yourselves treasures in heaven, where moth and rust do not destroy, and where theives do not break in and steal. For where your treasure is, there your heart will be also.

Matthew 6:20-21

Riches

What do you count as riches my friend --

Love, joy, peace and life without end?

Are the things of the earth the things you hold dear?

Hold fast to true riches, and face life without fear.

In Heaven is where our treasures should be,

And oh the joy when Jesus we see.

For it is written: " 'He will command his angels concerning you, and they will lift you up in their hands, so that you will not strike your foot against a stone.' "

Matthew 4:6

Angel

God sent me an angel
And I call her my sunshine.
She is my grandchild,
And I can call her mine.

God sent me an angel
And I call her my moonglow.
In the darkest hours of the night
She comforts with her glow.

God sent me an angel
And I call her my starlight.
I know that she is near me
As she twinkles in the night.

Shine, glow, twinkle,
My angel sent from God.

"Come, follow me," Jesus said, "and I will make you fishers of men."

Matthew 4:19

Jesus answered him, "I tell you the truth, today you will be with me in paradise."

Luke 23:43

Here I am! I stand at the door and knock. If anyone hears my voice and opens the door, I will go in and eat with him and he with me.

Revelation 3:20

Jesus

Today I met my Savior by the Sea of Galilee,
And I knew my life was different when He said,
"Come follow me."
He said "I'll make you fishermen, but you will fish
for men; and you will tell them that I came to
ransom them from sin."

Today I met my Savior on a cold and lonely hill,
And I heard Him pray in agony to do His Father's
will.
I said, "Oh Lord, remember me", as I hung beside
Him on the tree; and now I know why He paid the
price, so we might dwell with Him in paradise.

Today I met my savior, He was knocking at my
heart's door; and now I have the perfect peace that
all the world longs for.
He is standing at your heart's door, knocking to
come in.
He'll fill your soul with joy and peace, and cleanse
you from your sin.

So Joseph also went up from the town of Nazareth in Galilee to Judea, to Bethlehem the town of David, because he belonged to the house and line of David.

Luke 2:4

He went there to register with Mary, who was pledged to be married to him.

Luke 2:5a

...And she gave birth to her first born, a son. She wrapped him in strips of cloth and placed him in a manger, because there was no room for them in the inn.

Luke 2:7

It Began In Bethlehem

A star herald my Savior's birth,
And angels sang to men on earth.

There is a sea called Galilee,
And my Savior walked beside that sea.

There is a hill called Calvary,
And there my Savior died for me.

Someday I want to walk beside
that sea,
And climb the hill where he died
for me;

And sing with the angels upon
high,
In song it's call ed the 'Sweet
By and By.'

I thank my God for every remembrance of you.

Philippians 1:3

Acknowledgements

My gratitude for the love, forgiveness, mercy, kindness and guidance of my Savior.

My thanks to the pastors of my church whose study, prayer and dedication to God's word have clarified the scriptures for me.

Also my thanks to my Christian family who have loved me in spite of my failures and shortcomings.

And especially to my daughter and son-in-law who have compiled and edited my work, and for believing in me.